ABSOLUTE BEGINNERS
Bass Guitar

Order No. AM970585

Written by Phil Mulford
Cover and text photographs by George Taylor
Other photographs courtesy of LFI/Redferns
Book design by Chloë Alexander

Printed in the EU

ISBN: 978-0-7119-8890-0

Visit Hal Leonard Online at
www.halleonard.com

Contact us:
Hal Leonard
7777 West Bluemound Road
Milwaukee, WI 53213
Email: info@halleonard.com

In Europe, contact:
Hal Leonard Europe Limited
42 Wigmore Street
Marylebone, London, W1U 2RY
Email: info@halleonardeurope.com

In Australia, contact:
Hal Leonard Australia Pty. Ltd.
4 Lentara Court
Cheltenham, Victoria, 3192 Australia
Email: info@halleonard.com.au

Contents

Introduction

This book will guide you through from the very first time you take your bass out of its case, right through to playing bass parts to complete songs.

Easy-to-follow instructions
will guide you through
• how to look after your bass
• how to tune it
• learning your first notes
• playing your first song

Play along with the backing track as you learn – the specially recorded audio will let you hear how the music should sound – then try playing the part yourself.

Practice regularly and often.
Twenty minutes every day is far better than two hours at the weekend with nothing inbetween.

Not only are you training your brain to understand how to play the bass, you are also teaching your muscles to memorise certain repeated actions.

At the back of this book you will find a section introducing some of the music available for bass. It will guide you to exactly the kind of music you want to play – whether it's a comprehensive tutorial series, rock licks, jazz and blues, easy-to-play tunes or "off the record" transcriptions, there's something there for all tastes.

Tuning Pegs

Neck

Frets

Scratchplate

Volume control

Pick-ups

Tone controls

Bridge

G
D
A
E

Track 1 on the CD gives you the correct notes for you to tune each string of your bass. You'll hear each of the bass's open strings in turn, starting with the bottom string.

You can alter the tightness (and therefore the pitch) of each string by twisting the tuning pegs at the top of the neck.

A bass can also be tuned with pitch-pipes, a tuning fork, an electronic tuner, or by tuning to another instrument such as a piano. Once one string is in tune the others can be tuned to it.

Let's assume the bottom E is correctly tuned. Hold down the 5th fret on that string to get an A.

Now play the open A string – they should sound the same. If the A string is higher or lower, tune it down a little or up until they are the same. As they get closer in pitch you may hear a strange oscillating or "beating" tone generated by the two notes. The oscillation rate decreases as the notes become closer in pitch.

Repeat the process at the 5th fret for the D string and G string.

E A D G	E A D G	E A D G	E A D G

▲ Tune E string

▲ Tune A string to E string

▲ Tune D string to A string

▲ Tune G string to D string

▲ Finger positions for tuning

Position and posture

In order to play well you must be comfortable with your instrument.

Holding the Bass
Start with your bass at about waist level, relaxing your shoulders by rolling them back a little.

Check your playing position in a mirror and compare it to the photos on these pages.

It's important to keep the neck of the bass pointing upward a little.

Mani
Stone Roses &
Primal Scream

Nicky Wire
Manic Street
Preachers

Sting

Which position?

Every bassist has a slightly different posture – just check out the photos of bassists used throughout this book to see the variety of possible playing positions. Experiment with the length of the strap until your left and right hands feel comfortable – a higher position may make playing slightly easier, but a low-slung bass often looks much cooler!

If you plan to play standing up for any length of time a good quality strap will help you avoid discomfort. A soft, wide strap is best, as the width helps to spread the weight of the instrument.

Plucking

You have two choices on how to produce notes on the bass: either

- pluck with the first two fingers (usually alternating)

or

- use a pick or plectrum

Pick or Fingers?

Your choice will probably depend on the type of music you want to play – if you want to play in a jazz or soul group, you should probably use your fingers. If, on the other hand, you want to play in a metal or rock band you'll need to use a plectrum to make yourself heard!

With Fingers

Using your first two fingers in an alternating style takes some practice. Start slowly. Then you can speed up and your playing will remain accurate.

Your thumb can be anchored on the bass, on the side of the pickup, the scratchplate or on the chrome pickup cover if your bass has one. The photos below show how your fingers should look.

▲▶ **Possible right hand plucking positions**

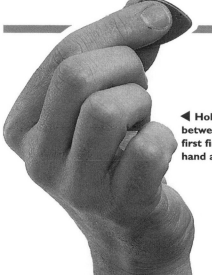

◀ Hold the pick firmly between your thumb and first finger, keeping your right hand and arm relaxed.

With a Pick

Picks come in different thicknesses – thin, medium or heavy. Each gives a different sound and feels different when playing. For bass, heavy picks tend to be best as they are less likely to flex as you hit the strings.

Practise striking the open strings of your bass with the pick – you can strike the string once on the way towards the floor (a "downstroke") and again on the way back up (an "upstroke").
Try to hit the string with the same force on the way down and on the way up – this will ensure that you get an even feel.

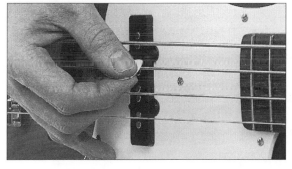

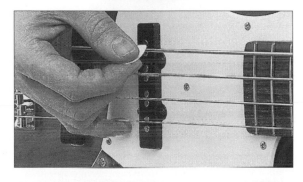

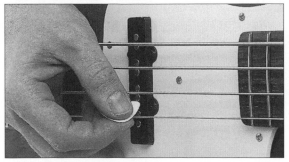

◀ Starting a downstroke on each string ▲ Playing with the pick

Left hand position

Place your left hand over the fretboard, with your thumb on the back of the neck roughly behind your middle finger.

You should always aim to use one finger per fret – practise stretching your fingers, as shown in the photo. If you find this a difficult stretch on the lower frets, try the same position above the 5th fret, where the frets are closer together.

The photo below demonstrates a poor hand position – notice how the fingers are all bunched together.

Using one finger per fret may seem tiring at first – but persevere and you will soon build up strength in your hand. If you feel your hand getting tired, take it off the fretboard, let your arm hang down by your side and relax completely. You should never continue practising if your hand is hurting as it can cause permanent damage.

▶ **Paul McCartney – possibly the most famous left-handed bassist of all time.**

Tip

The left-handed guitarist

Left handed players should simply reverse all the instructions in this book – your fretting hand will be the right hand, and your plucking hand will be the left.

Red Hot Chili Peppers' bassist Flea is known for performing backward somersaults while playing his bass!

First steps

Here's your first piece, laid out on the standard music stave and with a system called tablature.

The Stave
Traditionally, music is written on five lines, called a "stave". On these lines and spaces notes are written, indicating pitch and rhythm.

If a note is too high or too low for the stave an extra short line is added, called a "leger" line.

The important leger line note for bass is the one that represents the lowest E.

Check out the diagram below to see how different notes are represented on the stave.

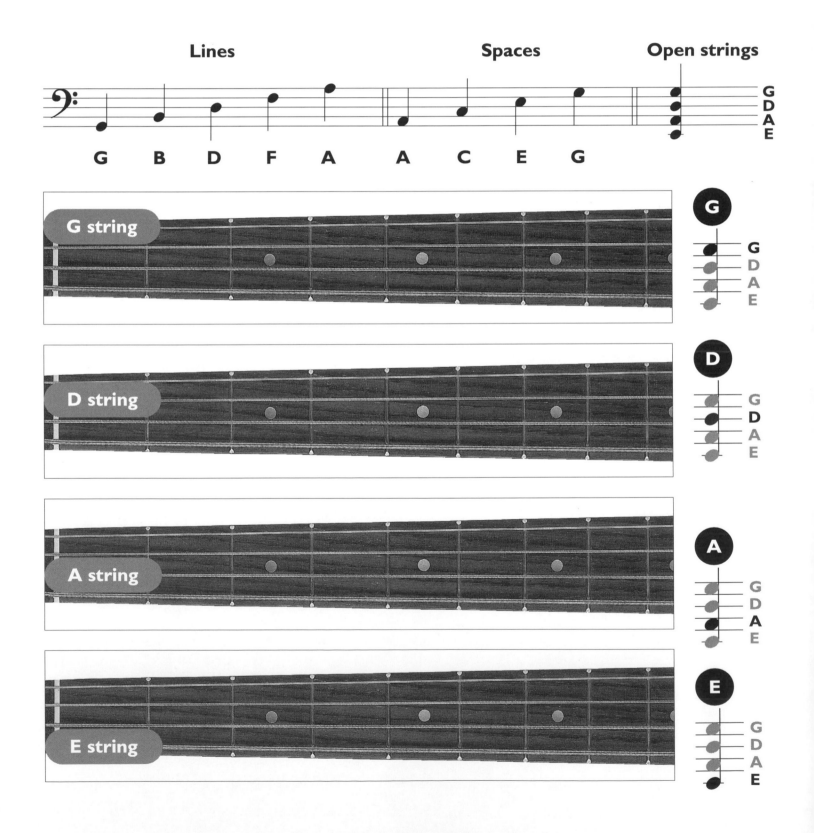

The good news for bassists is that you don't need to worry about the musical stave, because "tablature" will tell you exactly where to find each note on the fretboard. Tablature (or TAB) is always given under the traditional musical notation.

The four horizontal lines represent the four strings of your bass. The lowest line represents the bottom string, and the highest the top string.

The numbers on the horizontal lines tell you exactly which string and which fret you need to produce the note that you want! The only thing that TAB can't give you is the rhythm – you'll still need to refer to the stave for that.

Try finding some of the notes indicated by the TAB in this example:

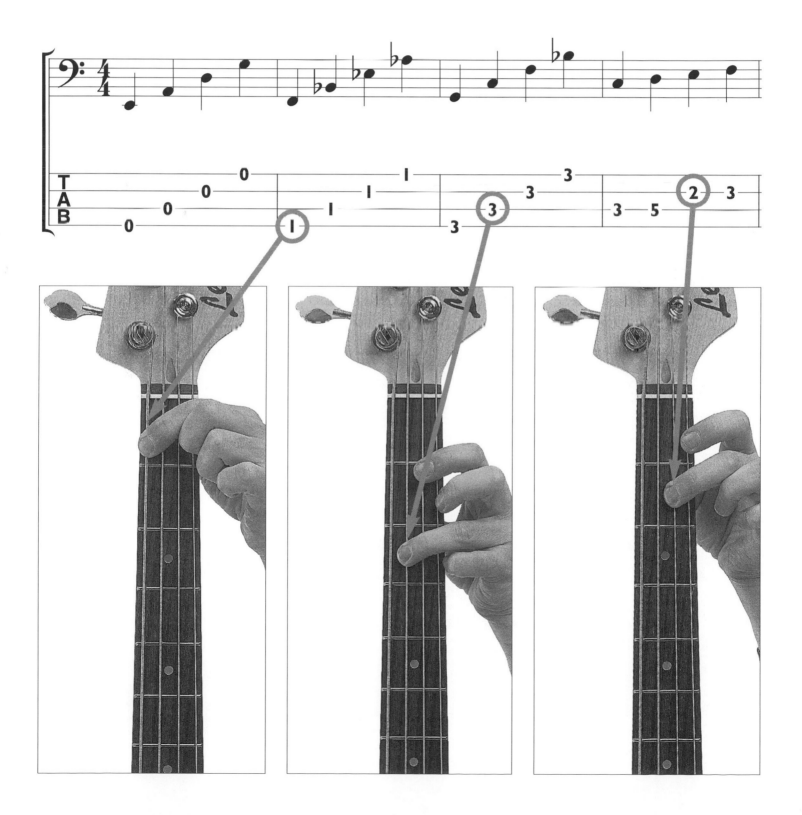

Your first note A

Let's start straight away with your first bass line – this track can be played all the way through using one open string!

Listen to **Track 2** to hear how the bass fits in with the rest of the band – it simply plays the open A string (the 3rd string) on the first beat of each bar. The drummer's bass (or kick) drum is also struck on this beat, so listen to that and try and hit your note at exactly the same time.

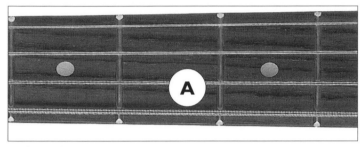

▲ **Open A string**

Rhythmically, the note you are playing is known as a crotchet or quarter-note. Count 1-2-3-4 as you play and then pluck or pick the open A string as you count "1". Play the note for one beat only, then stop it by resting your finger on it as you count "2".

Once you're familiar with the tune, try playing along with **Track 3** – remember to play rhythmically and with confidence – it's your role to provide the foundation of the track, so you've got to be rock steady!

Song structure
This tune has 3 sections:
Sections A and C are identical, so we'll call them the *Verse* sections
Section B has a different harmony, so we'll call that the *Middle* section.

The rhythm section
The bass player and the drummer together form what is known as the "rhythm section" – they lock together to provide a steady pulse over which the rest of the band can play. Get into the habit of listening carefully to how drummers and bassists work together to produce a groove.

▼ **Led Zeppelin's rhythm section – John Paul Jones on bass and John Bonham on drums.**

♩=112

A **Verse**

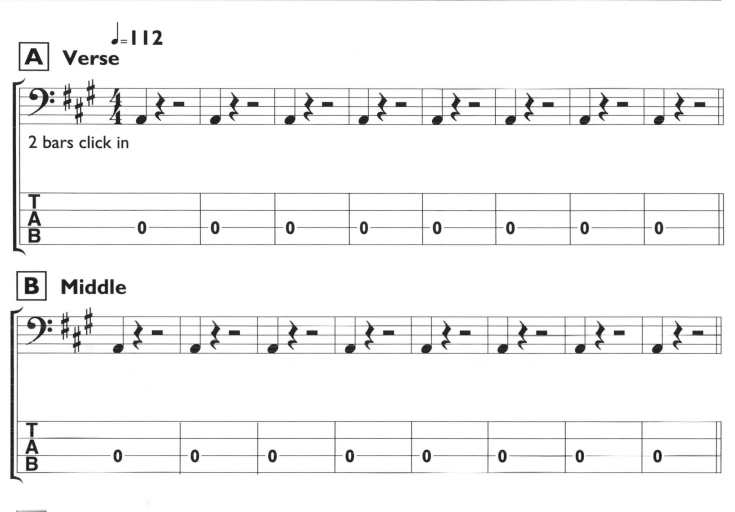

2 bars click in

B **Middle**

C **Verse**

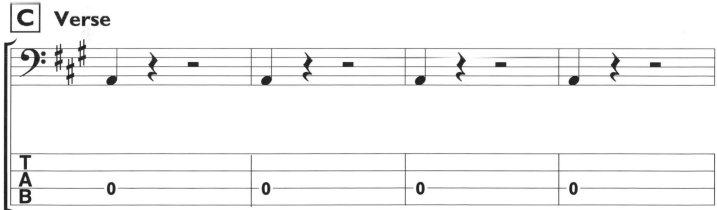

From A to E

This second tune moves from the open A string to the open bottom string E.

Instead of only playing on the first beat, you're now going to play on each of the four beats in the bar. Once again, the bass drum is struck on each of these beats – so listen out for it and try and lock in exactly with that rhythm. As you're not using your fretting hand to hold down notes, this is an ideal opportunity to concentrate on what your plucking hand is doing. Experiment with alternate down/up strokes with the pick, or pluck with your first and second fingers.

Whichever method you use, try to make sure that you keep the notes separate and consistent in volume.

Track 4 demonstrates how the bass part should sound.

Track 5 is your chance to play along.

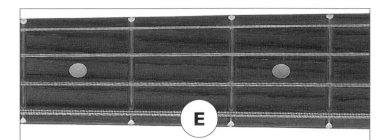

▲ **Open E string**

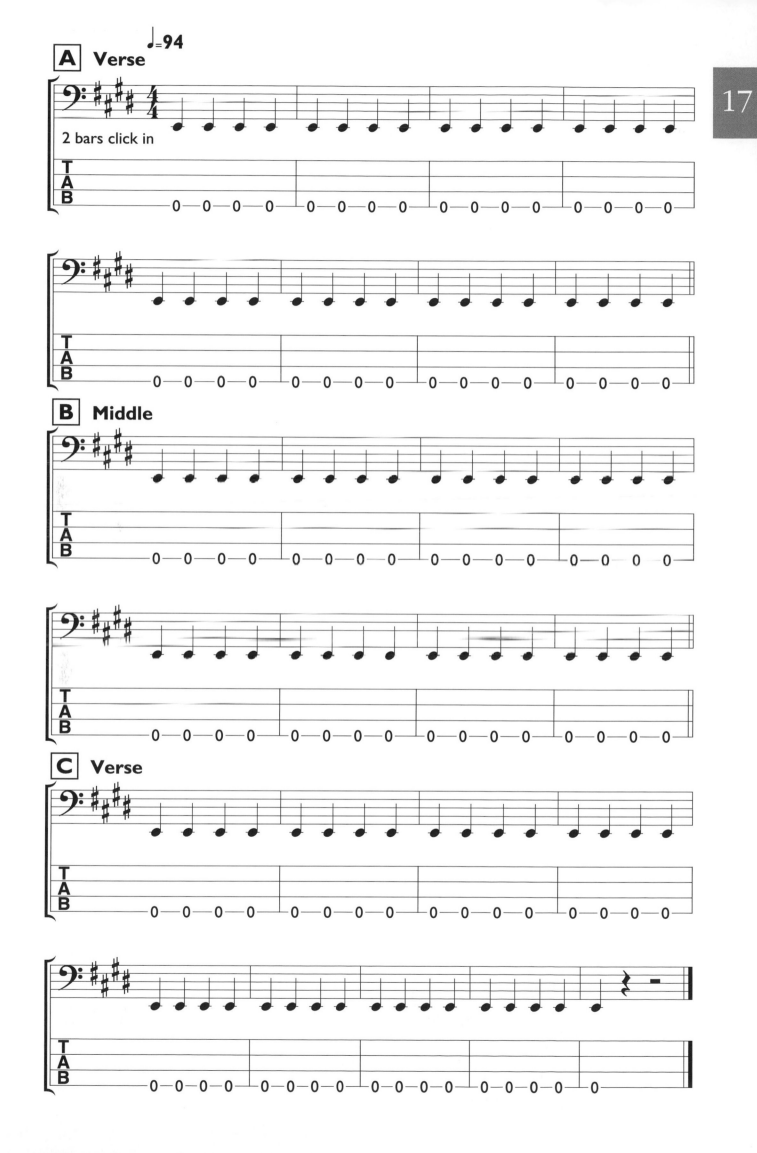

Speed up your learning

Some hints to help you practise:

1 Try to find time to practise every day – even if it's only for 10 minutes. It's much better to practise every day for 10 minutes than it is to practise once a week for two hours!

2 Listen and learn! Try to pick out the bass parts to your favourite tracks, and hear how the bass player fits in with the rest of the band.

3 Start slowly! Once you've perfected the part, you can then speed up – and your rhythm will remain steady.

You've used the bottom E and A strings – now it's time for the D string and a new rhythm.

This tune is a classic groove which you'll always find useful. It uses an eighth note or quaver as the second note in each bar. The quaver is half as long as a crotchet.

Listen to **Track 6** to hear how it sounds.

Count a steady four in a bar and try to play this rhythm - you should find that the quaver falls inbetween beats 2 and 3.

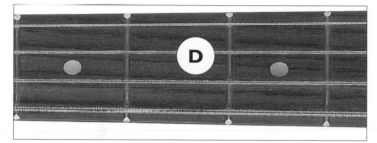

▲ Open D string

If you insert an "and" inbetween each beat as you count, you'll find it even easier to fit the quaver in:

1 & 2 **& 3** & 4 &

You should play on the beats underlined. Once you've mastered this rhythm, try playing along with **Track 7**.

This tune has an Intro (section A), with sections B , C and E as Verses, and D as a Middle for contrast.

Listen to the way that your bass notes sound different as the chords change over it.

Off-beats and syncopation
The "ands" that you've just been counting fall in-between the main beats of the bar, and are known as *off-beats*. Playing on off-beats makes a bass part much more interesting – in fact there's a special musical term for it – *syncopation*.

Right hand plucking position

♩=112

A **Intro**

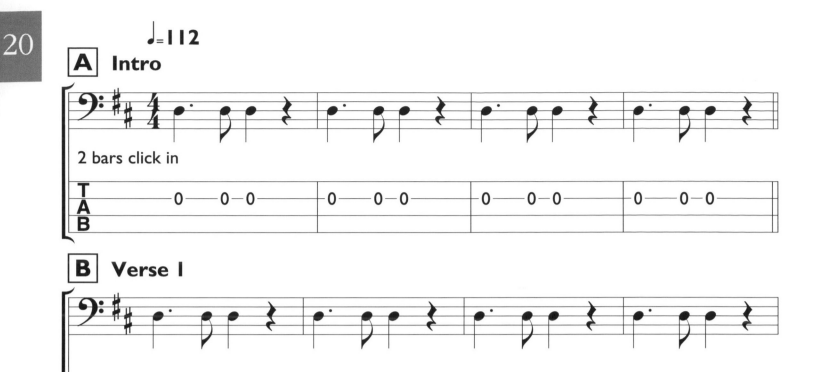

2 bars click in

B **Verse 1**

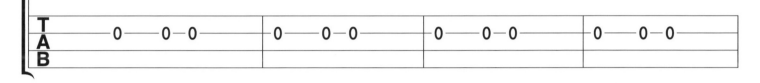

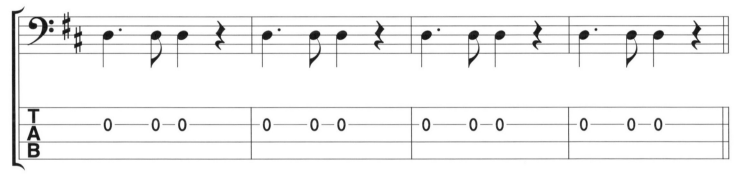

C **Verse 2**

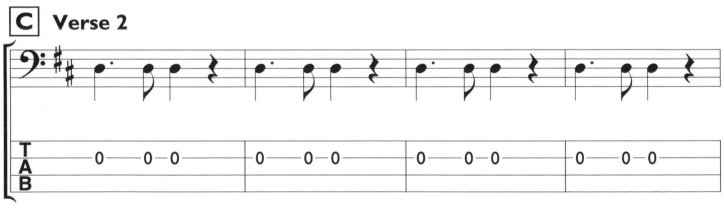

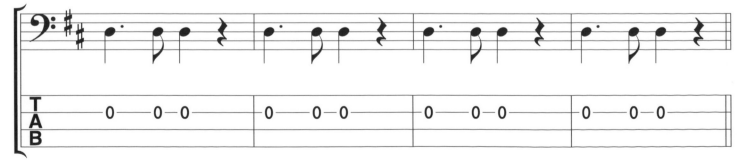

ABSOLUTE BEGINNERS
Guide To Bass

The Fingerboard

The Notes

Tablature

Tablature, or tab notation, runs in parallel with the standard stave, and gives additional information specific to the bass guitar. Think of it as a drawing of the neck of your bass, where the four horizontal lines represent the strings, the lowest line being for the E string, the highest being for the G string. The numbers written on these lines represent the fret positions on the fingerboard.

Notice that tab gives us only string and fret information. It doesn't tell us anything about rhythm, dynamics (loudness) or pitch as such.

Stave notation gives us a full musical picture, whereas tab is only an aid to playing the bass. Of course when you run the two in tandem you do get the complete picture.

Tuning

The first thing to do when you strap on your bass is to tune it. Nowadays it is normal to have an electronic tuning device of some kind, but it is still important for you to understand and to be able to tune it without an external reference. You will find this particularly useful when the battery in your electronic tuner goes flat!

Tuning By Harmonics

Harmonics, simply put, are a series of overtones which are present in any vibrating string. When fretting a harmonic, both portions of the string, behind and in front of the finger, must be free to vibrate. Therefore the finger is not actually pressed into the fingerboard, but simply rests lightly on the string.

Try this on frets 5 and 7 until you get a clear bell-like tone. The harmonic on the 5th fret on the E (lowest) string is the same harmonic as at the 7th fret on the A string. If you play them together you will have some idea of whether the strings are in tune with each other.

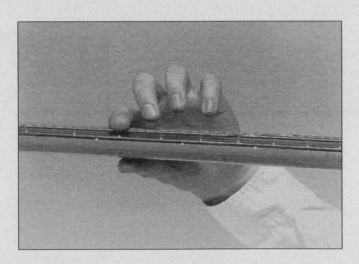

First of all you must check that the open E string (the string you start tuning from) is in tune with the other instruments, or the CD you are playing along with. Once you are satisfied that the E is in tune, you can play the harmonic at the 5th fret to check the next string. Let this harmonic ring and play the harmonic on the 7th fret of the A string.

The two harmonics will now be heard together. If they combine to make one pure tone you're in luck - they are in tune!

If there is an oscillation (a regular beating sound) going on between them the A string will have to be adjusted until there is a pure tone. If the oscillations are fast the notes are fairly wide apart.

The closer the tuning gets the slower the beating becomes. You have to judge whether the harmonic on the A string is higher or lower than the harmonic on the E string.

Once the A string is tuned to the E string you have to repeat the process twice, tuning the D string to the A string, and then the G string to the D string. When each harmonic at the 5th fret in tune with its adjacent higher string at the 7th fret, your bass is in tune.

Tuning By Full Notes

Harmonics are not the only way to tune your bass – you can use full notes as well. Firstly, tune your E string to a reference instrument or CD. Once again the low E becomes the reference point from which all other tuning is done.

Having tuned the low E we can tune the A string by playing an A on the 5th fret of the E string and comparing its tuning with that of the open E string. As before we will hear either a pure tone if the strings are in tune, or an oscillation if they are not.

As the notes draw closer together the oscillations (or ringing) will slow down gradually until they disappear completely, at which point the strings are in tune. The process is repeated for the rest of the strings.

Hand Positions

The Fretting Hand

First of all, relax your fretting hand - this is most important as a relaxed hand will prevent tension-related pain in the wrist and fingers.

Shake your hand and arm, allowing your arm to fall down by your side. Your hand will automatically assume a relaxed and natural position.

As a general rule it is good to use one finger for each fret, as pictured. Your fingers should be spaced out and relaxed, with the thumb behind the middle and index fingers.

Although this may help in the short term, bunching up your fingers in this way will prevent the development of individual finger strength, reach and flexibility.

There is no easy way to acquire a good technique. It is good practice to keep your 'spare' fretting fingers (i.e. those which are not actually fretting a note) in contact with the fingerboard at all times. This is a classical cello player's technique.

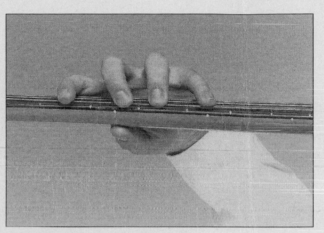

Move your hand to a playing position, as pictured. At first you may find it difficult to relax whilst applying pressure to the strings. This will improve as your hand and fingers gain strength. Don't bunch your fingers together in an attempt to exert the necessary pressure on the strings.

Holding The Bass

The height at which you hold the bass is a matter of personal choice, though it is true to say that for rock music the bass is slung low, while for funk and slap styles it is worn significantly higher.

There are no set rules to dictate where you should hold your bass, but be practical. Try to keep a relaxed posture with a straight back. Keep your shoulders back, otherwise you will suffer from fatigue and thereby shorten the time span during which you are able to play in comfort.

If you play standing up but practise sitting down, it is a good idea to still wear your strap when sitting. This will keep your bass in the same position, relative to your body, as when you are standing.

Methods Of Plucking:

Fingers

There is no set method for finger plucking, though it is obviously better to have some logic in your action rather than a random approach. You can use any or all of your fingers, though most people find it effective to use the first and second fingers, alternately. The third finger doesn't have the same independence of movement as the first two, and is better avoided until later.

The picture shows a typical example of the placement of your plucking hand. Try to anchor on something solid like the side of a pickup or the scratchplate. Practise playing the A (second lowest) string alternately with your first and second fingers.

Plectrum

The plectrum is a shaped piece of material, usually plastic or metal, which is used to pluck the strings of the bass. It comes in various thicknesses, or gauges, so you should be able to find one to suit your personal taste.

Because the plectrum is made of a material harder than the flesh of your fingers, the sound it produces from the bass is more sharply defined. This is especially popular in rock styles where a hard-edged 'clicky' sound is needed to kick the music along.

D Middle

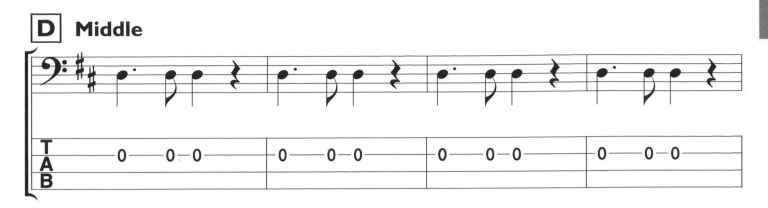

E Verse 3

Your first 12-bar blues

Next up, let's play some blues.

This 12-bar chord sequence has been used for thousands of songs in blues, pop, rock and many other types of music – once you're familiar with it you'll start to recognise it everywhere.

Here we're going to take the bass rhythm from the previous tune and play the open string which relates to each chord.

The first four bars are on A, so that's what we play. In bar 5 the chord changes to D, so we change to D too – and so on. The whole 12-bar sequence can be played with just the open E, A and D strings.

Listen to **Track 8**

and then play along with **Track 9**.

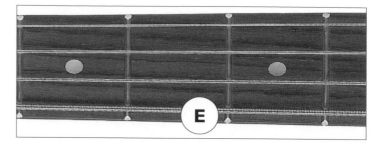

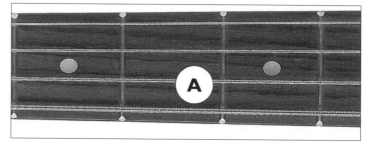

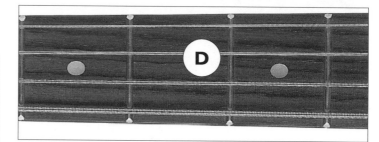

Tip

If you get tired, take a break, let your plucking hand relax and then try again. As you practise you'll build up more strength in your hands, and you'll be able to play for longer.

▼ **Cream (bassist Jack Bruce, drummer Ginger Baker and guitarist Eric Clapton) prepare to tackle another 12-bar blues.**

2 bars click in

The symbol 𝄇 at the end of bar 12 is known as the repeat sign – once you reach that sign you should return to the beginning of the example and start again. The second time through ignore the sign and go on to the last bar.

CHECKPOINT

WHAT YOU'VE ACHIEVED SO FAR...

You can now:
- Position your right and left hands properly
- Pluck or pick the strings
- Tune your bass
- Read simple TAB
- Play the open E, A and D strings
- Play bass lines in time with a backing track
- Understand simple off-beat rhythms

Playing with both hands

So far you've only used open strings – now it's time to put your fretting hand into action.

Finding your way

All musicians practice sequences of notes known as scales to give them greater finger strength, speed and flexibility – and bassists are no exception.

The diagram on the right shows the fretboard pattern for a C major scale.

C major

• All major scales consist of 7 notes – C major uses the notes C D E F G A and B.
• C major is named after the note that it starts on – C!
• The major scale forms a particular pattern on the fretboard – you'll soon come across other patterns such as the *minor* and the *pentatonic*.

Listen to **Track 10** and follow the TAB given below – this is known as the scale of C major.

Play each note four times in a bar, along with the drum groove (**Track 11**).
Use alternate first finger / second finger plucking or alternate strokes of the pick.

▼ **Starting position for C major scale**

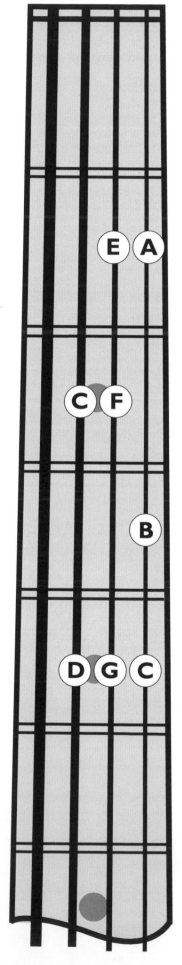

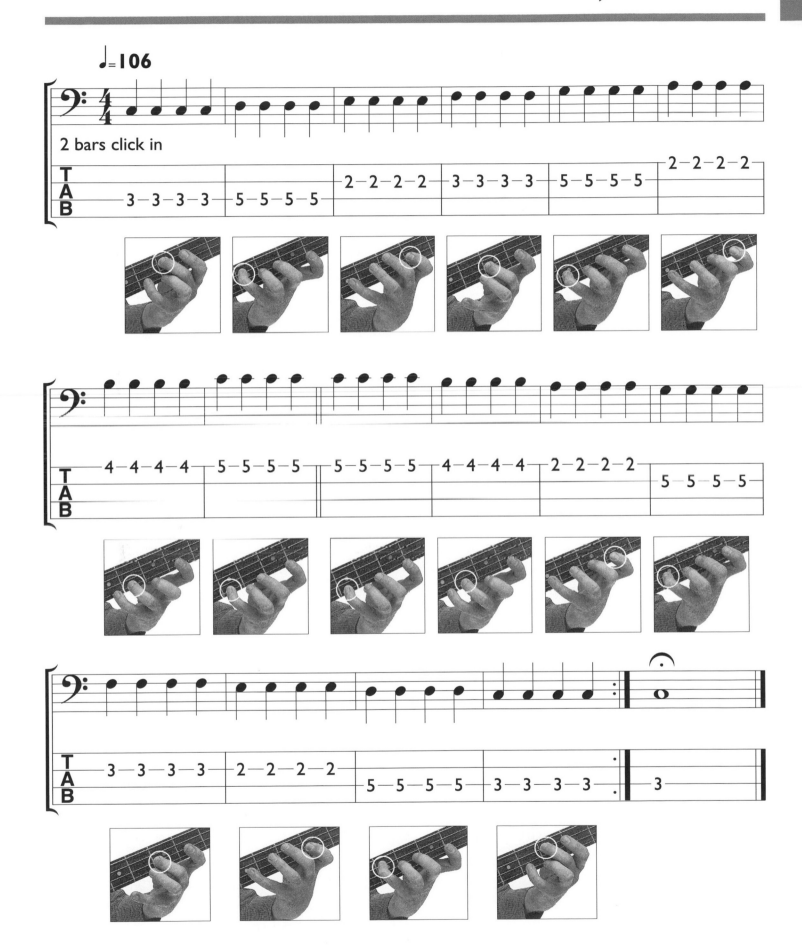

Speed it up!

Now we're going to take the same finger pattern but play each note only once.

Listen to **Track 12** to hear how this should sound.

You'll have to think quickly to be able to play this in time – start slowly and gradually build up speed, until you're ready to play along with **Track 13**.

So far, all the bass lines you've played have used root notes – they're the bottom notes of the chords under which you're playing.

But you can also use the other notes of those chords to spice up your bass lines...

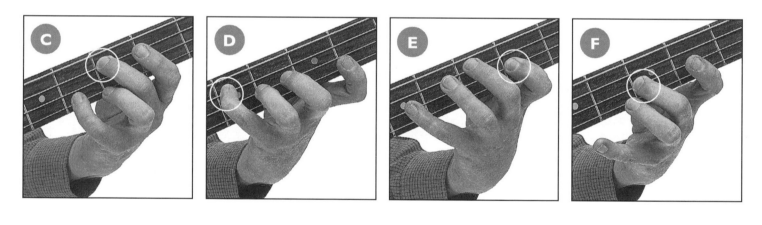

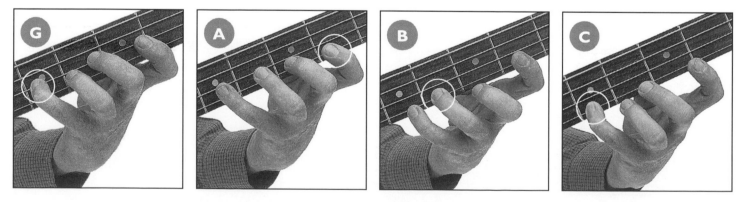

An arpeggio of C major is created when we play the 1st, 3rd, 5th and then the 8th note of the C major scale: C E G and then C again.

The example below (**Track 14**) shows you how to play this arpeggio, based on the C major scale pattern you learned previously.

Refer to the fingerings shown in the photos – start slowly and build up speed until you can play along with **Track 15**.

Movable patterns

Because you're not playing any open strings this pattern can be moved to any position on the neck – it's known as a movable pattern.

This means that if you wanted a D major arpeggio you could just move the whole pattern up two frets. In fact, using this pattern you can play any major chord shape you want!

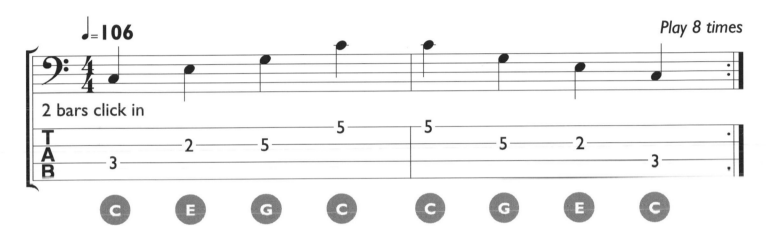

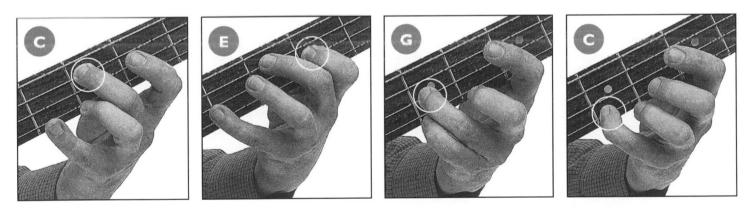

Chords & Arpeggios

When a guitarist plays a chord – he (or she) is generally playing at least 3 different notes simultaneously. Try this on your bass – it doesn't sound great, does it? The lower pitch of the bass guitar means that chords just don't sound very good. But if you split chords up and play each note separately you create an arpeggio – and they are ideal for creating bass lines.

Tip

The top two notes can be played either with your third and fourth finger, or by using the little finger to hold both notes down on the first and second strings.

Minor arpeggios

You can do the exactly the same thing with minor chords. The example below gives you an arpeggio of A minor, starting on the bottom E string.

Listen to **Track 16** – try to hear the difference between this minor pattern, and the major pattern you've just played.

Minor chords have a much darker, gloomy sound – in contrast to the bright feel of a major chord.

Once again, start very slowly and work out exactly where your fingers should fall- then gradually speed up until you can play along with **Track 17**.

Tip

This is also a movable pattern. Simply move the shape up or down the fretboard to get any minor arpeggio you want.

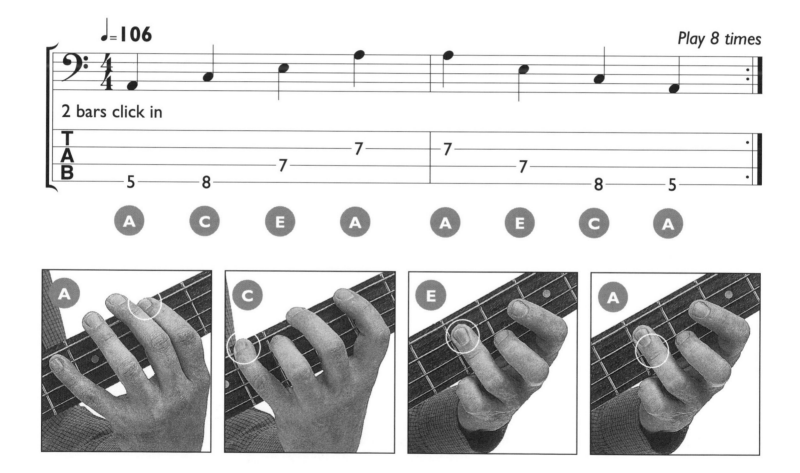

▲ Left hand position

Let's give your fretting hand a rest, and concentrate on your plucking hand.

This example will really test your stamina!

There's only one note to worry about here – a low G – the challenge will be to keep the rhythm steady and even.

Listen to **Track 18** to hear what it should sound like!

When you're happy with your right hand technique, try playing along with **Track 19**.

You're playing eighth notes (quavers) so there are 8 in each bar – two on each beat. Count 1 & 2 & 3 & 4 & steadily through each bar and pluck/pick steadily – aim to produce an even volume on each note.

▲ Right hand plucking position

▲ Right hand picking position

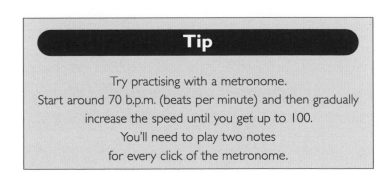

Tip

Try practising with a metronome.
Start around 70 b.p.m. (beats per minute) and then gradually
increase the speed until you get up to 100.
You'll need to play two notes
for every click of the metronome.

2 bars click in

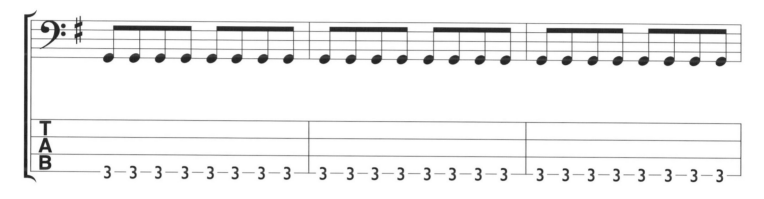

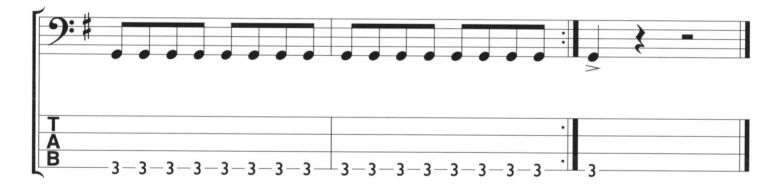

Make sure that your left hand and arm don't become tense – relax and let your arm hang naturally.

Here's another example to test your stamina, this time using the note B♭ on the first fret of the 3rd string.

Track 20 gives you a demonstration.

Track 21 is the backing track.

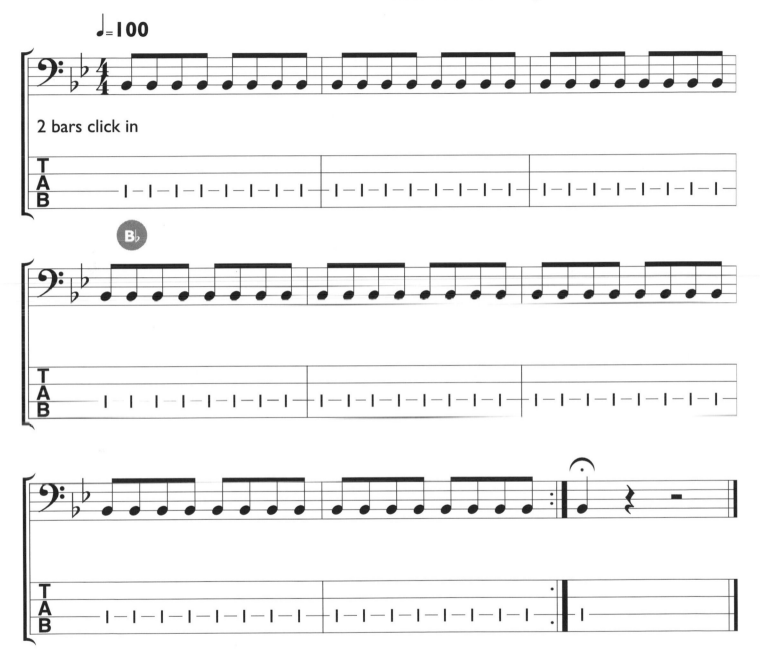

2 bars click in

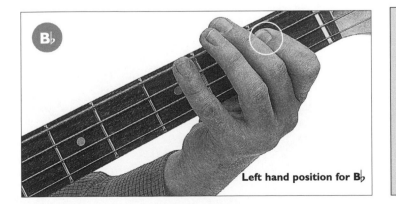

Left hand position for B♭

CHECKPOINT

WHAT YOU'VE ACHIEVED SO FAR...

You can now:
- Play a major scale pattern
- Play major and minor arpeggios
- Maintain steady plucking rhythms at fast speeds

Playing songs

To finish, we're going to apply all the basic ideas you've learned to a couple of tunes.

The first example is a midtempo "down-home" blues. It has a shuffle feel, as if each beat is dividing into three rather than two – listen to **Track 22** – you'll recognise this rhythm straightaway.

The example is a 12-bar in the key of E – you tackled a blues in A back on page 23 so you should be familiar with the structure.

Note that the chords for each bar are written above the stave – this helps you to know which notes you could play other than just the root note.

Use the arpeggio exercise to work out where you can play A, D and E as arpeggio figures and then experiment putting them in the right bars.

1st & 2nd time bars

The symbol ⫶‖ at the end of bar 12 is known as the repeat sign – once you reach that sign you should return to the beginning of the example and start again. Now, check out the brackets above bars 11 and 12 – these tell you that you should use those bars on the first and second times through the blues only – this will lead you to the repeat sign once more – so return to the top for the third and final time. On the third time you need to leave out the 1st and 2nd time bars and skip straight to the 3rd time bar, which will take you to the end of the piece – otherwise you'll end up going round and round in circles!

Once you're confident with the changes, try playing along with **Track 23**.

▼ **P-Funk's Bootsy Collins – one of the funkiest bassists of all time.**

Tip

Watch out for the last bar of the 12 – it's a little bit more complicated. Isolate that bar and practise it slowly – it's a classic blues phrase that's used to round off the piece.

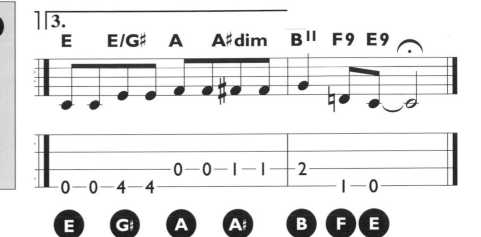

see photographs below for finger positions

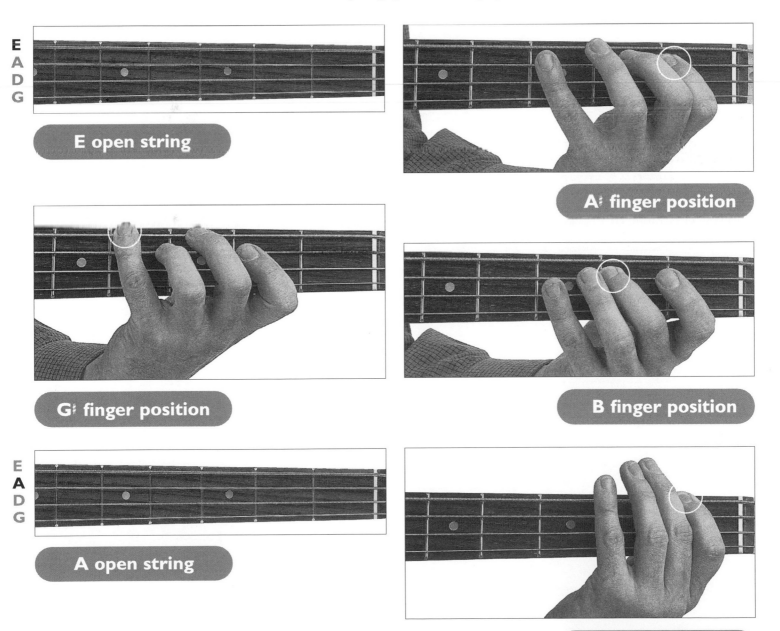

E open string

A♯ finger position

G♯ finger position

B finger position

A open string

F finger position

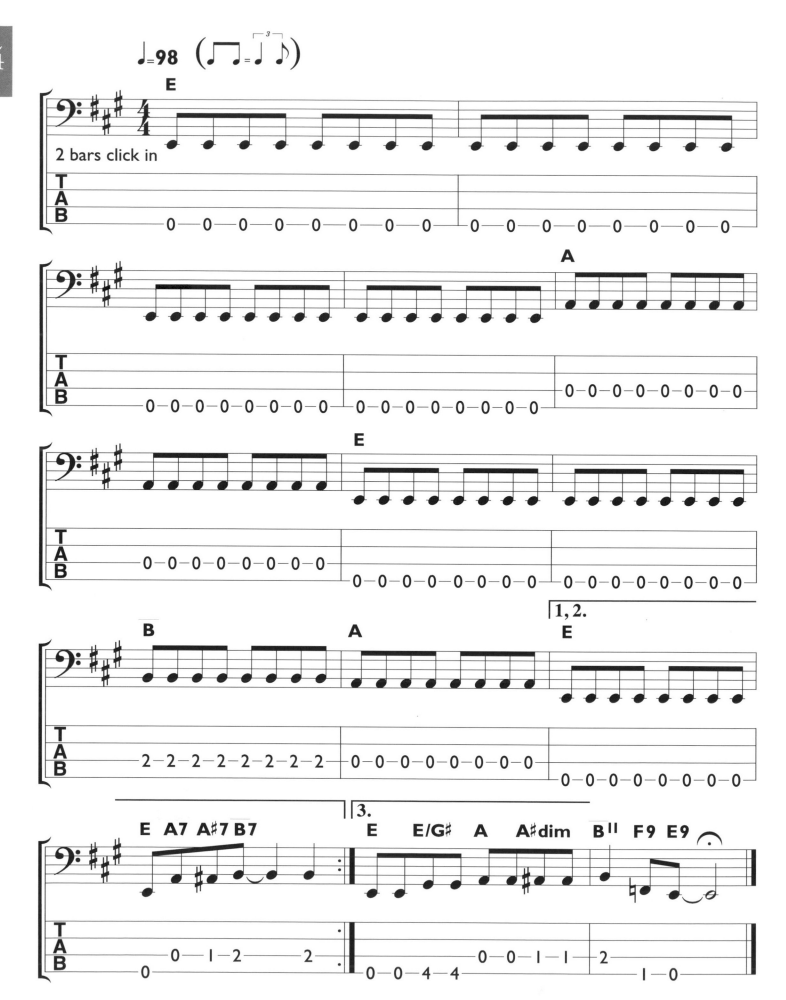

This last tune is a much longer rock number in the key of G.

It has a four-bar intro before you come in on bass – listen to **Track 24** and try to familiarise yourself with the structure of the song (like the previous example, it uses first and second time bars).

The first 4 bars of the track don't have a bass part - so count carefully and be ready to come in at letter A.

The Verse section uses the following 5 notes - if you follow the fingerings indicated in these photos you should find that they fall under your fingers easily.

When you reach section B you'll find the bass part breaks into "pumping" eighth notes.

Section B uses exactly the same finger positions as the verse.

Section C is a repeat of the intro but this time you do join in. You then play sections A and B again, (with the second time ending), which will then take you to section E, the outro.

Here are the fret and finger positions for section E.

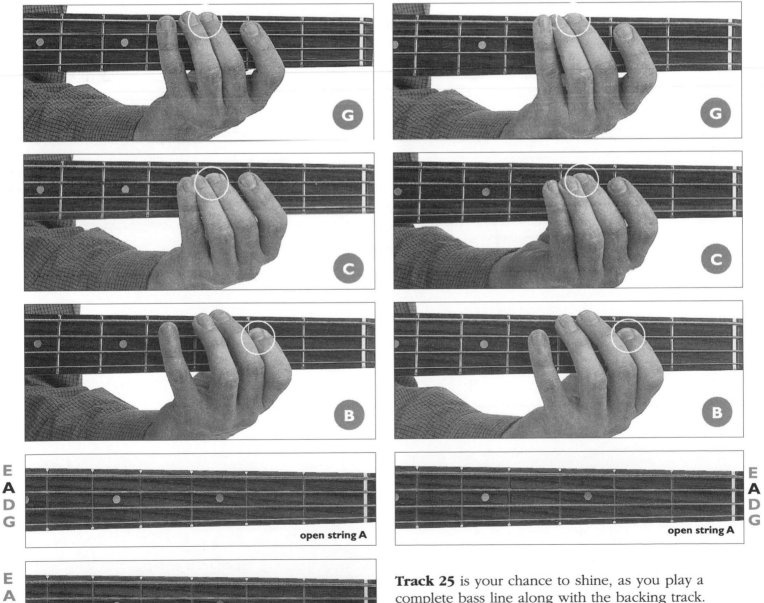

Track 25 is your chance to shine, as you play a complete bass line along with the backing track.

Let it rock!

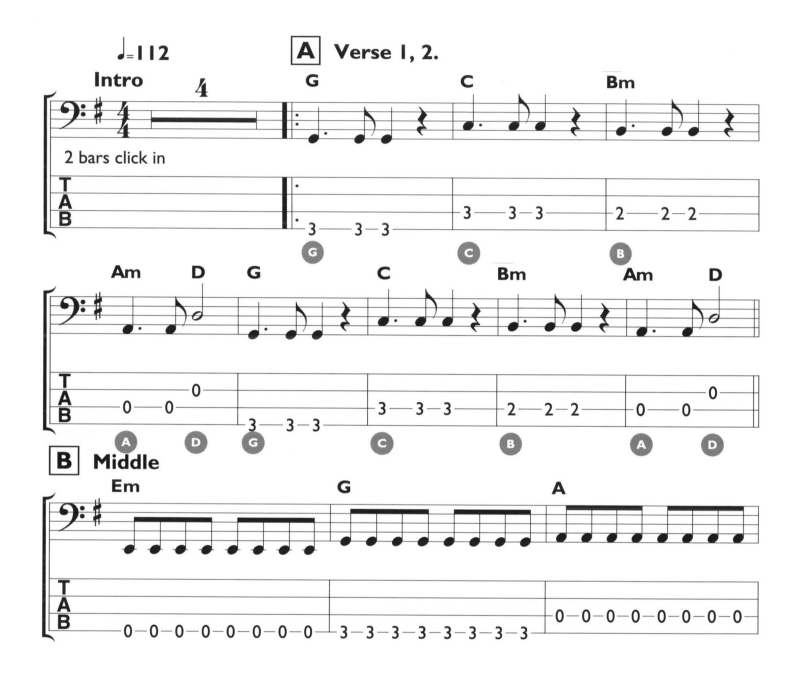

Tip

Watch out for bars 8 and 12 where the
chord changes half-way through the bar – try
to think ahead, and be prepared for each
chord change before it happens.

Congratulations!

You've made a good start in bass playing. The skills and techniques you've learnt in this book will form the foundation of your bass playing in the future.

If you want to take your bass playing further then check out some of the books listed on page 40, and spend some time listening to the bass playing of the musicians featured in this book.

FINAL CHECKPOINT

You've now covered all the basics of bass playing. You can:

- Tune your bass
- Read tablature
- Play scales and arpeggios
- Play 12-bar sequences in A and E
- Play fast repeated 8th note and syncopated rhythms
- Play complete bass lines to two songs

The Who's **John Entwistle** and **Roger Daltrey**

Alex James
Blur

Mani
Stone Roses

Here are some classic, but simple, basslines, that you should now be able to approach. Most are simple enough to pick up straight off the record!

Another One Bites The Dust Queen
Design For Life Manic Street Preachers
Parklife Blur
Shakermaker Oasis
She Bangs The Drums Stone Roses
Smoke On The Water Deep Purple
Walking On The Moon Sting
With Or Without You U2
You Really Got Me The Kinks

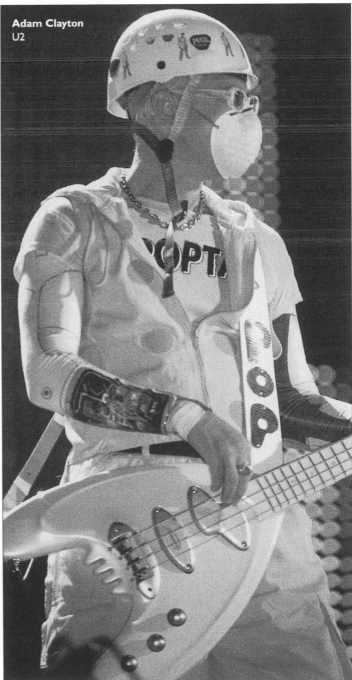

Adam Clayton
U2

Further reading

If you want to learn more, here are some other great books that will take you further into the world of bass:

Rockschool

The eight Rockschool grades are divided into four zones – Entry, Player, Performer and Pro. The packs have standard notation and tablature plus great sounding CDs featuring top musicians. Rockschool grades are accredited by Trinity College London, giving a measure of achievement that is recognised around the world.

Entry Zone
Debut Bass, along with Grade 1, is for players who are just starting out and who are looking to build a solid technical and stylistic foundation for their playing.
RSK019909/RSK019910

Player Zone
Grade 2, along with Grade 3, is for those who are building on key skills to express their musical personality across a range of styles.
RSK019911/RSK019912

Performer Zone
Grade 4, along with Grade 5, is for those who are confident in all the key skills and who are stepping up to more advanced skills and stylistic expression.
RSK019913/RSK019914

Pro Zone
Grade 6, along with Grade 8, is for those who are ready to stretch and refine their playing at an advanced level of technique and musical expression
RSK019915/RSK019916.

FastForward

An exciting series of book/CD packs, including complete music for all riffs, licks, hints and tips. The accompanying CD lets you listen and play along to the audio tracks. Discover the secrets of authentic rock bass styles, playing as you learn with the pro-quality CD backing tracks.

Classic Metal Bass
Music in the style of Metallica, AC/DC and Black Sabbath.
AM92429
Metal Bass Styles
Play in the style of Guns N'Roses, Metallica and others.
AM92428
Rock Steady Bass
The sounds of Status Quo, The Police, Tina Turner and others.
AM92425

The Complete Bass Player

The easiest, rockiest, most comprehensive guide to playing bass, in two books by Phil Mulford. Uses both standard notation and tablature and features play-along tracks on the accompanying CDs.
AM91109/AM91110